January, 1988

To Don and Marjorie,
Dear friends of many years.
Love,
Olena Mae

Philippians 1:3-6.

EVAN D. WELSH

A Touch of Heaven Here

Edited by Dr. Mark Fackler

Tyndale House Publishers, Inc.
Wheaton, Illinois

First printing, April 1985

Library of Congress Catalog Card Number 84-52526
ISBN 0-8423-7294-6
Copyright 1985 by Olena Mae Welsh
Printed in the United States of America

CONTENTS

FOREWORD

Children who grow up in Christian faith have received a kind of special grace, and churches which nurture children bear a difficult responsibility. Children, after all, need a variety of teachers and elders: realists who refuse to romanticize the faith, idealists who hold firm to the vision.

I was born the year Evan Welsh left College Church in Wheaton to take a pastorate on Plymouth Road near downtown Detroit. There at Ward Memorial Presbyterian Church, this youngster met furloughing missionaries who taught Sunday school, workingmen who passed out candy after church, faithful women who taught summertime Bible classes, and a pastor who was able to connect with all of them, including me.

Eight years into life, I sat in the crowded Ward Church sanctuary while a tearful congregation bade farewell to a tearful pastor and his wife. Evan Welsh had preached the Word, administered the sacraments, and lived the faith uniquely. Now he was to become the first chaplain of Wheaton College. It was not an evening for dry eyes. Such was the rare connection he made in that place.

It was twenty years before I saw him again, yet certain memories are indelible. So when I read these sermons on prayer, there is yet fire and passion and a sand-and-gravel voice behind them: God's gift to a young boy.

Mark Fackler
Wheaton College Graduate School

ACKNOWLEDGMENTS

It would be difficult for me to adequately express appreciation to all the many beloved friends of ours who have encouraged me to write about Evan's life. It all started with the firm urging of Dr. and Mrs. Kenneth Hansen to simply write down episodes from the rich life of sharing and ministry God gave us. Others, too numerous to mention, also encouraged me to write.

However, when we discovered tapes of Evan's own messages from the Okoboji Lakes Bible and Missionary Conference, we decided to save my memoirs for another time and let Evan's own words and thoughts occupy these pages. Dr. Robert Brown, director of the Conference, graciously made those tapes available to us.

With valuable assistance from Dr. Mark Fackler of the communications faculty of Wheaton College, these sermons, once given to a small and dedicated group of believers in Iowa, may now reach beyond to a wider audience. On occasion, we included some of my memoir material to illustrate the seven messages here. I am deeply grateful for the assistance of Mr. Kenneth Petersen of Tyndale House Publishers and also for the help of the Wheaton Alumni Office. Their timely help turned this work from pages in a binder to pages in a book.

Finally, I would like to add a few words of tribute to the man himself, Evan Welsh. As his wife of thirty-five years, I could not help but sense the validity of his own personal walk with God. His life was lived constantly in the atmosphere of prayer and dependence on Jesus Christ. The overflow of such a relationship was countless expressions of love and concern to those with whom he came in contact.

May you, the reader, catch something of the excitement he shared in these messages about the joy as well as the responsibility of daily fellowship with God.

Olena Mae Welsh
November 5, 1984

INTRODUCTION

I have a certain love affair with books like this, for they bring to life words that we thought were lost, words of a man of God who deserves to be heard. Evan Welsh never had time to write a book while he was living, for he was always counseling, helping, comforting, and being a friend.

For twenty-six years Evan worked with students and alumni at Wheaton College, first as college chaplain, then as chaplain of the Alumni Association. I worked closely with him for several years, especially when I served as president of the Alumni Association.

It was a magnificent experience to meet Evan, even in a casual encounter on campus. His face glowed with that easy smile, and he stepped forward with outstretched hands. For the next few moments I was the most important person in the world to him, and remained so until one of us had to leave. But that's the way he was with everyone.

Evan must have lived in the presence of Christ for he carried that presence with him. I always felt when I was with him that I had moved close to the person of the risen Lord. Evan didn't have to say anything. It was enough that he was there.

Evan first came to Wheaton in 1921 when his father became pastor of College Church. Twelve years later, Evan accepted the call to be pastor of the same church and remained there for thirteen years. In 1946 he became pastor of the 1700-member Ward Memorial Presbyterian Church in Detroit, where he served until 1955, when he returned to Wheaton as chaplain.

During his years at Wheaton Evan gave himself completely to minister to others. Someone told me that he had seen Evan take his watch from his wrist and give it to a young man who needed it more. When our son was killed in an auto accident, Evan and Olena Mae were among the first to come to our house. This was less than three months before Evan died.

Ed Coray, a close friend for sixty years, said, "Evan's spiritual children are almost like the sands of the sea. They are scattered worldwide." One of these is Torrey Johnson, founder of Youth For Christ, who was brought to a right relationship with Christ through Evan's witness and encouragement.

Billy Graham said, "I knew him for more than thirty-five years and considered him to be one of the godliest men I have ever known. His cheery smile, his warm handshake, and his constant encouragement affected my life very deeply."

In reading the words that Evan Welsh left behind, you will surely capture something of the spirit of this man. He is a man to be heard, for he has walked with God.

V. Gilbert Beers, Editor, *Christianity Today*

ONE

PRAYING FOR PEOPLE IN TROUBLE
GENESIS 18

Our loving God,
we could not live without prayer.
We thank Thee for the marvelous way
Thou dost fit Thy Word to our needs.
It may be a verse shared by a friend.
It may be the morning Scripture lesson.
As miraculously as You inspired the
Scripture is the way You fit it to our needs
in daily living, You who are all loving.
Amen.

DID you ever go to a dead prayer meeting? The pastor gets up and asks for praise notes or prayer requests. Then follows that long period of silence before someone speaks up: "Willie, our neighbor boy, broke his arm." People pause for a moment, stare with grave concern at the floor, and pray for Willie. Then someone says, "Mrs. Jones' aunt had an appendicitis operation." The people pause another moment to let the news of this health report take firm hold of their spirit, and wonder what kind of an aunt Mrs. Jones could have and where Mrs. Jones herself might be living now. Then someone prays for her. And so the meeting goes, from health news to the building committee to the Sunday school, and maybe someone mentions the prayer meeting itself.

God is interested. The hairs of our head are all numbered. No need is too small for our Lord to give an attentive ear. But here in a world exploding with vicious hatreds of all kinds, with people fearing nuclear holocaust, with others fearing to leave their homes at night and sometimes (God help our families) to go home at night, there seems to be little passion in our praying, little heartfelt burden.

The older we grow, the less we feel inclined to judge our brethren, so I'm not coming down hard on the cottage prayer meetings which don't get beyond Willie's arm and Bertha's aunt. Lots of folks today are bearing heavy burdens and just don't feel the exuberance of the Lord. But from my reading of Scripture, when a group of God's people meets to pray, their praise to the Savior and prayer for his help and guidance should be a passionate thing.

Abraham had passion. He wasn't hot-blooded every time, but he always trusted God for help with the really big problems. And he had as many reasons as any modern believer to get humdrum about the faith. Our text introduces Abraham sitting at the flap of his tent entertaining himself by watching the oak trees grow, and no doubt wondering, too, about this matter of the promised son. Yet behind this man's wind-glazed eyes is a mind alive with passion for his faithful God, a heart that looked beyond his own immediate needs, even beyond his own deepest longings for the promise, to the needs of people in the vicious city of Sodom. Here is Abraham's great prayer on behalf of Lot and his family and any righteous person that could be, might be, in that wicked city. Here is Abraham—that outstanding example of faith—rising to the needs of souls he does not know and to the deepest needs of his nephew Lot.

Did you ever tell a white lie? I don't believe there are colors to lies, as if some are okay if the lie is a lighter hue. I have sometimes had to go to a person when a comment or offhand remark I have made was not true. Sometimes I have been caught off guard and reflexively said the wrong thing. The Lord has made me go back to that person and admit that what I said was not true, not accurate. I feel a breach with that friend until the truth is made clear, until we get the peace of truth between us.

God always speaks truth, even when the truth is odd or hurts to hear. So when the angels remind Abraham, and Sarah too (listening from the inside of the tent), that the promised son is indeed God's plan for them and that the baby will arrive a year hence or so, Sarah laughs. And then she is caught in a lie, because she fears to own up to the embarrassing admission. The men were guests at her tent, after all, and they seemed to be pretty sure of themselves. So she said, "I didn't laugh." But the angel replied, "Oh, yes you did." Later on, as sure as the words of God are true, Isaac was born. His name means laughter. The connection between Sarah's laughter and the birth of another promised son is too ironic and humorous to miss. In Luke 2, other angels announce, "Fear not, for, behold, I bring you good tidings of great joy, which shall be to all people. For unto you is born this day in the city of David a Saviour, which is Christ the Lord."

Their appetites appeased, the heavenly visitors turned toward Sodom, and Abraham went with them along the way to the city. At that point in the story we are given a rare insight into God's regard for his servant Abraham. The text tells us that "the Lord said," but we don't know to whom these words were spoken, and they sound and read as if they were the thoughts in God's mind and not a conversation at all.

First we learn that the Lord decides to tell Abraham what his intentions for Sodom are; the Lord reveals his intentions to Abraham because He has chosen this man to carry the covenant promise. Abraham is truthworthy and responsible. God can trust him with information that would shatter and confuse other men. And then we learn that the heavenly visitors are on a kind of fact-finding mission to verify all the many reports of Sodom's sinfulness. That's a strange thing for angels to do, as if they had to corroborate information with the same techniques men are limited to using.

God knew what was going on in Sodom. But many times in the Old Testament and in the New, God accommodates himself to our finite ways by using human terms to describe his actions and his power. This literary device is called an "anthropomorphism" for the Greek *anthropos*, or man. When we humanize a lesson or a story to make its meaning clearer, we anthropomorphize something that is really quite above and beyond human knowledge. And that is happening here, for these agents of God hardly needed to trek from the territory of Mamre to Sodom to verify the evil cries reaching heaven's all-knowing God.

Another situation occurring here is "theophany," an appearance of the Lord himself. There are so many thrilling theophanies in the Old Testament: Adam and Eve, Jacob wrestling at the Jabbok, Gideon seeing the captain of our salvation. Then Abraham here with these three men, and he turns to one of them, and addresses his question. How the great Abraham knew that his visitor was God in the flesh, I do not know. But I am convinced that in the Old Testament, when the Lord appeared, it was Christ, the second Person of the Trinity.

Well, remarkable Abraham knew it was God in the flesh before him . . . a theophany. And he begins one of the most dramatic interrogations ever recorded. Of course, I don't mean a courtroom-style interrogation in which the attorney presses witnesses to prove the truth of their words. Abraham never questions the truth of God and never presumes to question God's wisdom or the rightness of the intended destruction of the city. No, this interrogation is really a prayer, a most dramatic appeal on behalf of souls Abraham did not know personally, but for whom he felt the passion of godly love.

Abraham was such a man of faith, and of action. The two qualities are really inseparable. True faith issues in righteous action. Weak faith or a false faith never puts feet and sweat and sacrifice behind the words. Take Hebrews 11. There's more action in that chapter than in any other in all of Scripture. Men and women of faith, real faith, are people of action.

Abraham was such a person, so when he felt the passion for souls in Sodom and heard of the imminent judgment facing the city, he opened his mouth and spoke out in a vital prayer on its behalf.

Abraham was also a sentimental person. I never felt it so keenly as when I reviewed parts of Genesis recently. Abraham was born in Ur of the Chaldees, a region in the Fertile Crescent—solid pagan territory. He was somehow of semitic lineage, a descendant of Noah, Methuselah, Enoch, Seth, and the original man and woman—the godly line. Abraham retained something of the covenant promises that go back to Genesis 9:15, though we can't imagine and don't know how he did it. But God appeared to him and called him, and he obediently took his family and started out on the trail of faith that brought him near the oak trees of this doomed and vile city.

Now his family was decimated. Abraham was one of the three sons of Terah. Haran, Abraham's brother, had died. Haran's son Lot had very obviously been taken into Abraham's inner family. Lot was to his uncle like a beloved son. So Abraham, his surviving brother, Lot, Sarah, and others in the growing party, made their way toward the land of promise, to Haran. There they stayed until Terah died. Then they moved down into the land of Palestine, and at Bethel Abraham built an altar and called on the name of the ever-living God.

He had grown in possessions, and so had Lot. Remember in Genesis 13 when herdsmen were having trouble finding grazing land for all the animals, and Abraham's greatness comes through, his magnanimity, for he says to Lot, "Let there be no strife between us, for we be brethren. You take the land you want, I'll take what's left."

Abraham would not let divisiveness spoil the family, as so often happens today among the people of God. He had the godly agape love. I could just see him putting his hands on the lad's shoulder. "You take the part you want and I'll take what's left." Not a very good business decision, but Abraham's business was caring for the family, even for the beloved son of his deceased brother. But at this point Lot slipped. He looked at the watered plain over there in the direction of Sodom and Gomorrah, and he pitched his tent toward Sodom.

Abraham had often been in a position to look out for Lot, to care about this troubled nephew. Lot went toward Sodom, though the city's wickedness grieved his soul (as we learn in 2 Peter 2:7). Abraham, too, must have grieved over the problems Lot brought upon himself by that compromising decision.

Yet the Lord honors Abraham. God reminds him of grace and promise that no earthly trouble could take away—by reminding Abraham of the covenant promise given to him. And just after that Abraham must risk life and limb, even though he is an old man, to chase down the four kings who had taken Lot captive in battle against Sodom. So with 318 armed servants, Abraham galloped after the enemy, defeated them, rescued Lot, his family, and his possessions, and had that mysterious meeting with wonderful Melchizedek, who is certainly a type of our blessed Lord.

I recall Tom, a fine student whom I got to know soon after taking the post of chaplain at Wheaton College. Tom finished college, went on to work for a while, and then called me one day. He was back in town, and wanted to have lunch. We met, and he told me how the Lord had called him to Ecuador. This was following the martyrdom of the five missionaries there in the mid-1950s. Tom wondered if he should pursue this sense of call to Central America, to Ecuador, to resume some of the work left by the five who died. I encouraged him, but advised he get training in his field before he go overseas. By God's grace, the Wheaton Christian High School had an opening in languages, and Tom fit right in. Students loved him, and wanted him to stay, but after a year or two Tom followed this word from God and accepted a position with radio HCJB. He and his lovely wife went down there, and they had a family. Then a terrible thing happened. His son Tommy was struck by a hit-and-run driver. But through it all Tom's faith grew and his work prospered. Not knowing all the answers, he had traveled the long road with his Lord. Tom's story could be told by many others as well, each one a blessed recounting of God's grace under trial and of His faithfulness for the journey.

Abraham's concern for Lot! Risking his life, no doubt, to go and rescue his nephew's son. Then came this particular experience with the three heavenly visitors: two angels and one a theophany, the

Lord Jesus himself. Abraham knows that he is talking to God. God tells Abraham what He is going to do. And then Abraham offers this marvelous prayer.

Reading some portions of Scripture, we do have to smile. This is too serious to call humorous, but the argument between Abraham and God has a comical side: fifty, forty-five, forty, thirty, twenty, ten, the argument goes. May I say it reverently—although it is serious business—the Lord must have smiled as He talked to Abraham. Spurgeon said that God loves men who argue with Him. Abraham had every reason to consider Lot a self-seeker who had made a bad mistake, but he is so concerned for Lot that he prays fervently, he argues with God, until he gets the bargain down to ten righteous men.

I asked myself as I read this again: Evan, do you pray for souls, for loved ones, who are facing temporal judgment, and eternal loss of their souls, with anything resembling Abraham's kind of concern? The prayer challenges me; it rebukes me.

I had an uncle Clarence, now with the Lord, who grew up on a farm in Kansas. As a young man he would ride into town every Sunday for church. A group of other young fellows in town looked down on this country boy, made fun of him. The hazing turned Clarence against Christ despite a godly father and mother. He left Kansas for Northwestern University in Chicago and made the football team, was Sigma Chi, married well. But he turned his back on God and embraced theosophy. If I wanted to get him angry, I just had to mention the blood of Christ. He would say something like, "That's immoral. I'm a good man. I don't need that."

He lived into his eighties, an unsaved man. But my grandmother, his mother, who lived to be eighty-eight, had calluses on her knees from praying for Clarence. My mother and I also prayed for him and felt that he would be saved. The last weeks of his life, he was led to Christ in the hospital by a Pentecostal neighbor, who wrote Mother, "You have every reason to believe that your brother died a saved man." Grandma had never given up; Mother never gave up.

Abraham prayed through, and Lot was spared. Abraham had plenty of his own concerns and needs, yet followed through for Lot. Abraham had a wife's disbelief to contend with, yet believed for her and for his family when their faith was low. And Abraham was not caught short of courage when duty called him to risk life and limb for his nephew. Through it all his prayers ring true and bold. I want to pray with that kind of passion.

TWO

GOD'S GLORY IN THE CRISIS PRAYER

EXODUS 32

*Dear God, we thank Thee
for placing in our hands the sword of the
Spirit and the gift of prayer.
You have given us, our Father, these
fundamentals of our faith,
these weapons of our warfare. And with them,
the ability to appreciate the life
that comes through their use. Make our lives
full in Christ today. Amen.*

IN a school we are supposed to learn. The children learning mathematics three blocks from my home at Franklin School are in the same business as older children at Blanchard Hall, just up the hill from our home. And for us older children yet, we still need school, we still need to learn and grow, and I suspect none of us will ever leave that part of childhood.

Many of you are experienced in the Word. I cannot assume to teach you anything when I speak and write in front of you. But I know that God's Word—every time I read it, when I really take time to read it and meditate on it—holds something new for me, something I had not seen before.

In Exodus 32 and 33, we come to another prayer from an Old Testament great: the prayer of Moses. Actually there are four prayers in these two narrative chapters. And unlike some of the prayers we study and certainly most we ourselves offer, Moses here is praying for God. He is primarily concerned for the glory of God. The great lesson that comes to me as I read these two chapters is Moses' complete identification with God's purposes.

The history recorded here is such an awful mixing of the true and the false. Here is false worship, the making and worship of a golden calf, and yet Aaron, who seems to live on both sides, gives a burnt offering and a peace offering after the heinous idol is broken. How often do we mix our Christian commitment with idolatry, even simple and explainable idolatry, the kind everyone around us is doing.

I was talking with a man the other day who is living with a woman not his wife. I urged him to consider God's way, but he was not going to break off that wrong relationship. He claimed he was doing a lot of good. He had a responsible job with many people reporting to him. So he could, in fact, do much good on the job and in other ways. I told him it was the devil's trick to get us to bargain with God. We know that such behavior is wrong. It violates God's purposes for intimate relationships, and ultimately, no matter what short-term benefits may appear to be attractive, the people involved are hurt deeply. We do not turn away from God's plan for living and from His moral standards without paying a terrible price. In this case, the man was resting on his claim of doing much good for the Lord, in a way he hoped would balance the scale. But we know —and I trust he really knows—that God wants us to come all the way to Him.

It is sad to read of the idol worship begun there at the base of Mount Sinai. The consequences of that idol plagued Israel for so long, and yet mixed up in that sin was a spark of the true.

We have here another case of that phenomenon we encountered in Genesis 18: anthropomorphism, where we use very human terms to speak of God. The Bible teaches us clearly that God is not a man, that He should repent. God does not need to repent, as if He were accountable to us for His behavior. But sometimes in Scripture we find words that are normally used to describe you and me, in our finiteness, to help us understand something of the divine heart and movement.

When Jesus fed the five thousand (as told in John 6) he turned to Philip and asked how they could provide for so many. Surely Jesus knew what He was about to do, but asked the question to test Philip. And again in Luke 24, the Lord Jesus makes that marvelous appearance to the two weary disciples on the Emmaus road. Jesus expounded to them from Moses and all the way through the Scripture concerning Himself: His atoning death, His resurrection. We read that He made as though He were traveling, and they urged Him to stay, for the day was almost over. Jesus never intended to leave them, but wanted them to ask Him to stay. In these two chapters, God is training and testing his special servants.

Moses had come to an intimate relationship with God. He was close enough to speak with God on the mountain as a man would speak with a friend. Oswald Chambers once said, "God does not have favorites, but he does have intimates." And David reminds us: "The secret of the Lord is with them that fear him, and he will show them his covenant" (Psalm 25:14). I am convinced, dear friends, that while God differs in the talents He has given—to some so much greater talents than others—God loves every person, God has a plan for every life, and God wants to be intimate with every one of us. Our various circumstances and intelligences do not matter a wink at the point where God reaches to us in His genuine and steadfast love. Moses had grown in that loving intimacy more than most of us do, and here Moses speaks with God on the mountain as you and I might speak to an intimate loved one.

Let's look at the three parts of Moses' prayer.

Verse 11. He reminds God that Israel is His creation, and that Israel was delivered from Egyptian bondage only by the power of God Himself. Only God could have done it. He reminds God of what He has done in the past, and where Israel stood in relationship to God. Moses rehearses the power and might of God. The impossible had occurred: a powerless people had been freed from the greedy Egyptian pharaoh. Only God could do this.

Verse 12. Here Moses reminds God that back in Egypt, God's name would be brought down. Yes, their God, the one they talked so much about, the one Moses talked about. The God who took them out into the wilderness—was it only to slay them? God's good name was very dear to Moses. So he reminds God of the gossip that will go on in Egypt if God judges them in this way.

Verse 13. Moses knew his Bible. Abraham, Isaac,

and Israel, the name given by God just after Jacob's great experience at Paddan Aram (Genesis 35). Israel means "prince of God, for you have prevailed with God and with men." Moses uses the term *Israel* to remind God of what God already knew. Moses knew the promises of God, and he knew that he was praying in the will of God when he made this great petition.

When you think of praying in a crisis, think of Moses here. Judgment is coming; the people had sinned. Moses' faithful leadership was being subverted by the stubbornness and sin of the nation of people following him. In contemporary terms, his ministry was close to ruin and the people under his charge were destroying themselves. A terrible hour of righteous judgment was fast approaching. And the Bible says that God heard Moses' prayer and "repented."

Now catch a vision of the scene. Moses comes down from the mountain and has his turn at getting angry. There he sees the people dancing and finds this awful golden calf, and Moses, great man that he had become, dashes the tablets of stone onto the ground. Then he calls for judgment. "Come over to the Lord's side," he calls to the people angrily and urgently. Levi was not the first-born, but there was a mysterious moving by the Spirit of God among the Levites, and the Levites stood forward as one man, and therefore they executed judgment on behalf of God and Moses. Because of that act the Levites were made the priestly tribe of the Old Testament.

Then Moses prays another of his great prayers, recorded in Exodus 32:30-33. Moses has become so identified with the work of the kingdom of God, with the purpose of God, and with the people to whom God had made promises through Abraham, Isaac, and Jacob that he says, "Now Lord, deliver this people. Lead them to the land of promise. But if not, blot my name out of thy book."

God's library, if you will, includes several books: the Book, the Word of God, the books that God keeps on the records of men, and then the Book of Life. In Revelation we read of the books being opened, when men stand before the judgment seat of God, and the judgment is visited upon those whose names are not in the Book of Life. So Moses says, "Lord, deliver this people. Lead them out. Forgive them. . . . But if not, blot my name out of thy book."

The great lesson here is that Moses was so identified with the purposes of God through His people and through the revelation he had been given, that he was willing to lay his life on the line, even his soul, that God's purpose should not be defeated.

One dear minister's wife told me how hard she had worked in a church, and the work was not conspicuously successful. There were heartaches. But she said that God had taught her a great lesson. As she looked back years later, she realized how much of her effort was for her husband's success. She wasn't working for souls or the glory of God or the good of Christ's church. She was working for Bruce and herself.

I'll be very honest with you. I never dreamed that God would give me the privilege of fifty-two years in the ministry, so far. How I would like to rewrite some of those chapters. There are times when I know the energy of the flesh predominated, when my concern was more for personal success than it was for the glory of God and for the souls of men. I hope that in the process of my growth in grace there comes the time when I'm not concerned what men think of me. As a Christian and as a person I want their friendship, their well-wishes. But the thing I long for—that I want to long for until all other considerations vanish—is the glory of God. I want to pray for people like Moses prayed, because God loves people, and because God works through prayer.

I heard one time of a London minister who had a church near Spurgeon's. This fellow was a famous minister, too. His devotional books are still in wide use. From his neighboring church this minister would see crowds of carriages rolling up to Spurgeon's Tabernacle. The minister was jealous, envious, and it nearly threw him, until he prayed through to victory, and he could say on a Saturday night, "Oh God, bless the Tabernacle tomorrow, and bless the crowd that gathers there, and if it please you, give me the overflow." Do you wonder why his devotional books are still classics? "Give me the overflow."

I think of all the times when a dedicated servant of God, devoted to the purposes of God, had to pay the price for his or her convictions. Tommy

Sandlin was a dear friend I met during my pastorate at College Church. We had many wonderful times together, including some late-night prayers while Tommy was struggling through his calling to the ministry. Tommy stayed with it, finished seminary, and took a church in Texas, a beautiful part of the country. There he ministered the Word of God to a small flock. Tommy knew that the gospel was color-blind, and when his ministry began to reach across racial lines, his people became irritated. Like Moses on the mountain, Tommy stood for the purposes of God: racism was idolatry. And after a series of telephone calls threatening his and his family's lives, Tommy decided to leave. But after several years of ministry back in Illinois, Tommy returned to Texas. At the same church he had to leave so many years earlier, Tommy was offered the manse for a retirement home, if he would only return to pick up the witness he had begun there. So God was faithful to him and vindicated Tommy's stand.

The Apostle Paul said in Romans 9: "I could wish that myself were accursed from Christ for my brethren, my kinsmen according to the flesh." And the great John Knox prayed, "Give me Scotland, or I die." Oh, to be so identified with God, and with the purposes of God, that all the pettiness that threatens a church's witness—the jealousy, the envy—is blotted out. And we bless God when we see Him work in other lives. And our lives are on the altar, if He cares to use us. Oh, if the glory of God could ever be our foremost concern.

THREE

WHEN GUILT OVERTAKES US

PSALM 51

*Almighty God, speak through Thy Word,
and may each of us be able to carry
away lessons from Your infallible Word,
to guide us on our pilgrim way.
May we grow in its wisdom, and put to work
the lessons we have stored away.
In Jesus' precious name, and for His glory,
Amen.*

I RECENTLY received a copy of a letter that shocked me. In part it read: "I have long made the language of the 51st Psalm my own. . . . Rylands [the addressee], if I should pass away before you do, and you have influence to prevent it, be sure that no epitaph accompanies my name, such as 'Faithful Servant of God' and so on, for such words would only convey a false impression. I can only say, 'Hang my helpless soul on Thee.' [Signed] William Carey."

We don't know everything behind this letter written by a great man of God, except that Carey saw himself as a sinner before a holy God. That's why he wanted to go to the ends of the earth—why he went to India—because he knew that men and women were sinners and needed divine grace.

Will Rogers had such a marvelous way—an epigrammatic way—of saying a lot in a few words. He once said, "When I go from city to city, I pick up the paper on Saturday night and turn to the church page to see what the preachers are preaching on. When I see what the subjects are in the great downtown churches, I ask myself, where does the sinner go?"

The heart of the Christian gospel is the forgiveness of sin. Some people regard the incarnation as the central doctrine of the Christian faith. Actually, the incarnation is second to the doctrine of the atonement. The incarnation was ordered of God because of man's need of reconciliation with Him. For a holy God there had to be that atoning sacrifice. So the eternal Son of God was made flesh.

When you and I see the conditions in America today, we cry out for the conviction of sin that we find in Psalm 51. We remember, of course, the vivid story of how this Psalm came to be written. The Psalms are such a miracle of God—the way most of them were written, by David, that ten-talent man, that shepherd-warrior who is spoken of as "the man after God's own heart." And yet, tragically, David fell into great sin.

Second Samuel 11 begins with David staying home from war at a time when he should have been fighting the enemies of God. Inactivity is a dangerous playground for the devil. When you find yourself getting lazy about your duties, or listless about your calling in life and your responsibilities to those God has put within your charge, look out. Especially look out for rooftop daydreams. David got into trouble while walking upon the roof of his palace. He saw Bathsheba bathing, and he was overcome with lust. And he did what any oriental monarch could have done. He sent for her, had relations with her, and sent her home. Bad as that was, even worse was his arranging for the killing of Uriah, Bathsheba's husband. This Uriah was a Hittite, a foreigner, but he was one of those from the seven nations of Canaan that saw God at work in Israel, and had joined himself to the Israelite congregation. Yet David arranged for his murder.

The plot was no simple assassination. Even the mighty David could not resort to quick solutions. Rather, with Joab he planned a coverup, a reasonable explanation that would hide his own scheming. It nearly worked. Yet the eleventh chapter closes with just that little line: "But the thing displeased the Lord." Then in the twelfth chapter we have Nathan coming before David and telling him that story of the two men—one with many flocks and herds, the other with one little lamb that was like a child in his bosom. A visitor came through who needed entertainment. The host took the lamb from the poor man and had it killed and dressed to feed the guest. His only lamb. His most precious lamb. Upon hearing the story, David was so angry that he judged the host deserving of death. Then Nathan uttered those dramatic words, "Thou art the man." David cried out in his sin, confessing. And Nathan said, "You are forgiven. Your sin is covered."

Realizing the tremendous grace God had shown, David wrote these words of Psalm 51.

In the first five verses, the emphasis is on David's awareness of his guilt, his sin against Uriah, against

Bathsheba, and against Israel. But mostly against God.

Sin is always primarily against God. When Joseph was subjected to that terrible temptation by Potiphar's wife, he said, "How shall I sin against God, and my master?" He knew that we are all first accountable to God. Such accountability seems remote and unimportant to many people today. God, if He appears at all, is last on the list of those we have wronged. Perhaps we have a picture of God being so loving and gracious that He would never hold a grudge. But the fact remains that God positively despises sin. He is utterly offended and deeply grieved by sin. Sin is a slap in God's face, a mockery of His laws, a carelessness for the beauty of His world and the fragility of the people He dearly loves. All around us we see that failure to recognize that sin is primarily against our Creator and the Preserver and Redeemer of our lives.

I love verse 6. It speaks of our own intimate walk with God. We may deceive others, but we never deceive God. And unless our conscience is more seared than I think, we don't deceive ourselves either.

A little poem called "The Man in the Glass" decribes a man shaving in the morning. He looks at that man in the glass. He has received the praise of his fellows and achieved high position, but there is no truth in the inward part, and therefore no respect for that person reflected in the glass. God desires truth in the inward part.

Verse 7 has that beautiful reference to the Old

Testament sacrificial system. The hyssop weed was used to apply the blood in certain of the sacrifices that typified Christ. The sacrificial system of the Old Testament was not simply a fire escape, the means for a person to continue with an impenitent heart and offer all kinds of sacrifices. God does not delight in that. But when there is truth in the inward part, real penitence, then that sacrifice has meaning. And the same goes for you and for me. First John 1:9 is our great promise and we can't hold anything back.

I had occasion recently to go down to the county jail. There I met a young man from a Roman Catholic background who had fallen away from the church. He was living with his girl friend. He was using drugs. This young fellow had appeared a couple of times at my Sunday school class, brought by a local mission worker, but soon he dropped out. I called him one night to tell him I missed him. He insulted me over the phone with abusive language and false accusation. Soon after he was picked up by the police.

I went down to see him at the jail. Apparently the shock of confinement behind bars had brought him to. As I walked in, God seemed to be prompting me to ask him, "Have you really scraped the bottom of the barrel? Have you really made everything right with God?"

He told me of his Catholic rearing and that he was waiting for the priest to come over so he could get right with God. I agreed that a talk with the priest might do good. But he didn't need to wait

for the priest to experience forgiveness. We got out
1 John and read that wonderful first chapter all the
way through.

Suddenly he said to me, "I see it!" And he accepted Christ. When I called the next week he told
me that he had had a nice visit with the priest, but
had made things right with God in prayer and in
sincere repentance.

Once when I was young I heard my minister
father tell this story. At a congress of religions in
Chicago, representatives of different faiths told of
what their dogmas and creeds had to offer. Then
one man representing the Christian faith got up.
He said, "I want to ask you one thing. Will your
faith remove the spot from Lady Macbeth's hand?"
Shakespeare's character was oppressed with guilt,
symbolized by the spot that would not go away.
And so she cursed the spot—a futile gesture, because the guilt could not be absolved by anger.

Many futile gestures today replace God's way of
forgiveness. No, we cannot work our way out of
guilt. We cannot balance our way out of guilt, as if
forgiveness were the lot of those who spend some-
what more time each day doing good deeds over
bad ones. We cannot depend on religious ritual and
churchly pronouncements, from any quarter. And
we cannot declare ourselves "not guilty" as though
guilt were a psychological problem to be shed by
recovering a positive mental attitude.

The blood of Jesus cleanses from all sin. Blessed
be God, that He will always hear our prayer and
forgive our wrongdoing. Always.

FOUR

PRAYING AGAINST ALL CIRCUMSTANCES
DANIEL 9

*Dear God, we thank Thee
for the great admonitions to pray in Scripture,
and the illustrations given to us
of the power of prayer. In our own lives,
we can humbly say we've seen Thee
answer prayer again and again. Lead us in
the Holy Spirit, we ask for Jesus' sake.
Amen.*

THE superintendent for congregational churches in Missouri visited a town. The church was not doing very well. He talked with the deacons who wanted to meet with him. They said, "You've just got to get rid of this pastor of ours. We're not getting anywhere."

The superintendent replied, "Let me ask. Do you pray for your pastor every day?"

One of them said, "We didn't know we were supposed to do that every day."

The superintendent continued, "Well, you don't *have* to, but it would be a nice thing. Tell you what. I'll make a covenant with you. I'm too busy to handle this situation now, but I'll be back this way in a month. If every one of you deacons will promise to pray every day—really pray for your pastor—I'll come back in thirty days, and if things haven't changed, I'll move him. We'll get you someone else."

In thirty days he came back and met with the deacons. They said, "Let us alone. We've got the best pastor in town. We're having a revival."

That little story is not oversimplified. More things are wrought by prayer than this world dreams of.

The prophet Jeremiah told Israel that they were to go into their captivity willingly. They were to sow seed and build houses and give in marriage—regular life activities. They were to live as good citizens of the land of Babylon because their captivity was divine judgment. The king at the time, the arrogant and stubborn Zedekiah, refused to obey the words and warning of the prophet. The result was tragedy in his life and suffering for the people.

Daniel was taken captive along with so many others, and Daniel made good in the land of the captivity. All along, however, Daniel's heart was back in the holy city, in the place where God had placed his name. Also, Daniel pored over the Scripture. We don't know just how much of the blessed Word of God Daniel had, but somehow, some of the prophecies of Jeremiah had gotten through to the captives.

As he pored over the prophecies of Jeremiah, he realized that the seventy years were nearly over. Through Jeremiah, God had told His people that seventy years would pass over the land while they remained in Babylon. And then God said He would forgive and restore. " 'When seventy years are completed for Babylon, I will visit you, and I will fulfill my promise to bring you back to this place. For I know the plans I have for you,' " says the Lord, plans for welfare and not for evil, to give you a future and a hope' " (Jeremiah 29:10, 11).

Daniel read those words, and read the calendar, and felt that those seventy years were nearly over. God has told us to watch for the signs of the times, but He has left enough uncertain that we ought not commit the sin of date-setting. For example, the seventy-year captivity of Israel—did it start in 606 B.C. when Jerusalem first fell and was it fulfilled in 536 when the decree of Cyrus was given? Or did it run from 586 when the city actually was sacked and ruined and was then fulfilled in 516 when the foundation of the temple was laid?

God left a certain interplay of uncertainty, but He gave the main signs. Daniel knew that the time was coming for that promise to be fulfilled. Daniel prayed regularly, even though it nearly cost him his life. He prayed, we know. But this time, with the hope of the Lord newly alive in his heart and mind, he prayed with fervor and a new expectancy.

In verse 3, the phrase "prayer and supplications" seems redundant, but the word "prayer" is a broad one. The great theologian Warfield used to say that prayer has four elements: praise and adoration, thanksgiving, confession, and petition. But "supplication" is narrower. It means more specific, definite petition. Together they constitute the main and mighty source of strength for the spiritual battle we are called to fight.

Prayer and supplication are often associated with fasting and sackcloth and ashes. Sometimes we are led to fast. If we do, Jesus told us not to tell anybody about it, but just to anoint our face. Fasting is a secret thing between yourself and God. Not for outward display or for outward demonstrations of spirituality. Certainly not for winning the praise and attention of other believers. God desires truth in the inward part.

The opening words of the prayer are "Lord, we have sinned." One of Wheaton's greatest professors used to say, "I like Daniel. He wasn't afraid to say 'we' when he confessed sin on behalf of Israel. He didn't say, 'Those folks over there, what sinners they are.' " (Her name, by the way, was Elsie Storrs Dow, and she taught English for fifty years.) Daniel was one of the people, and he acknowledged personal responsibility.

Daniel began, "We have sinned. We've committed iniquity. We haven't harkened to the prophet." And then he realized the character of the God to whom he was praying in sackcloth and ashes, "O Lord, righteousness belongeth unto thee, but unto us confusion of face."

Now here is the bright note. To the Lord belongs righteousness, mercy, and forgiveness. He is the God of all grace, the God of all mercy.

Up to this time, apparently, Daniel had not sensed that his countrymen had bothered much to pray penitently or to tell God of their need for Him, even in their distress and dispersed condition. You and I feel that way so often in our own country. We read of the various nostrums proposed to deal with enormous problems, and yet so often we are turning to human theories instead of realizing that the bottom-line need is to be right with God. I have a deep conviction, and I know you do too, that if we as a nation got right with God, we would be strong, impregnable, able for God's time.

My father was overseas in World War I. Though in grade school, I followed the fortunes of the war closely and the peace that followed—Woodrow Wilson's going abroad seeking to bring about a just peace. But British leaders were still playing the old game: to the victor belongs the spoils. The result was the imposition of reparations against Germany that it could not possibly fulfill, until in its desperation the country was thrown into the arms of that awful demagogue Hitler.

I remember reading how reporters were eagerly waiting the result of the Versailles Treaty. At last the document was completed. One of the greatest reporters in Europe picked up a copy of the treaty and was so excited that he did not sit down while he read it through. For nearly an hour he pored over that document, then threw it down and said, "This means war." We fool ourselves thinking we know too much to look to God. Daniel underscores the common lesson: even in their sorrow the people had not called upon God, had not made their prayer to Him.

In verses 14 through 19, we see in Daniel just a little touch of Moses as he pled for Israel in Exodus 32. Both men were so identified with the purposes of God that they could pray their great prayers. Daniel prays to his Lord for the people's comfort that they may go back to the land of their nativity and know the comfort of beautiful, familiar surroundings. The basis here: "O Lord, forgive, . . . for thine own sake, O my God, for thy city: for thy city and thy people are called by thy name."

That's what we want to pray for as we pray with the glory of God in mind. We pray for the souls that are lost, we pray for the suffering that people are undergoing in our day. It isn't God's best will. But mostly we pray that the glory of God may come through in our own land.

I feel such a responsibility, and I know you do, as citizens in a world where God has blessed us so. As Olena Mae and I drove from Wheaton to Iowa a few days ago and saw the marvelous cornfields, I thought of the people who will die of starvation in this world today, twenty-eight every minute, according to one recent report. How blessed we are, how abundant our resources, and how much we do need to keep faith and never forget the source of our blessings.

Among my recent readings was a book on the history of evangelicalism in America. I have never felt so keenly our great heritage as a nation. The author went back to Jonathan Edwards, then to that great preacher who could be heard a mile, George Whitefield, and then on up through the early decades of America's independence. A great many of the leaders in America at that time—we talk about getting back to the faith of our fathers—had been touched by the rationalism of the French Enlightenment. There seems to be quite a lot of debate about the faith of these early leaders, and it is true that not all of them, by any means, were apologists for evangelical faith. But nearly to a man they had a high regard for God, for providence, and a conviction that the moral law was the most rational law and that man could discover it. Men like Jefferson and Lincoln were God-fearing men, and in many cases confessed Christian faith.

I remember the thrill of going down to Mt. Vernon a few years ago, and the unforgettable time Olena Mae and I had there. It was getting toward twilight and we came down from the beautiful mansion to the grave of George and Martha Washington. They are in a crypt barred by an iron gate, but you can see through the gate where the coffins are laid behind marble slabs. On top of the inscription is John 11:24-26 where Jesus said, "I am the resurrection, and the life: he that believeth in me, though he were dead, yet shall he live: and whosoever liveth and believeth in me shall never die." And I realized afresh something of the greatness of the faith of the father of our country. The mores of our society were shaped by God-fearing leadership. Our heritage is great.

You and I want to pray for God's forgiveness for our nation's neglect of His ways and His honor, for our growing disdain for authority and our loss of moral nerve. One of the most neglected portions in the Word of God is 1 Timothy 2:1-8, where the Scripture tells us to pray earnestly for those in authority, to raise up our leaders in prayer, that the glory of God may be upheld among the people.

Then let me remind you that Daniel's prayer was

made during a very low time in his people's history. Here they were under the thumb of the world's greatest empire. What chance did they have? How many stones would this Goliath take before he toppled? Too many, by any human judgment. Freedom and a return to the homeland and to the worship they had enjoyed there was a distant dream by any human measure. But Daniel took faith in God's promise of deliverance. And Daniel prayed in faith, repentently, humbly, confidently.

Let us pray that God will bless us with revival, that we could be a blessing to other nations. Let us pray as Daniel prayed.

FIVE

TOUCHING GOD IN PRAYER

DANIEL 10

Loving God, we thank Thee
that You have made life an upward climb,
and that the vista of heaven
and of life's wonderful portion grows
more beautiful as we ascend. Keep us
growing, Lord, all the way to
the perfect day. Amen.

PRAYER is sometimes hard, exhausting, and mysterious. I don't intend at all to belittle the many prayers which do not drain our energies—grace at meals and nighttime prayers with children and so many other common and meaningful times of addressing our Lord. But in this chapter Daniel faces the discipline of exhausting and mysterious confrontation with God.

The great W. B. Rylie used to say: "There are times when we say our prayers, and then there are times when we really pray." Isn't that true? My prayers can be desolutory and perfunctory, though not insincere, but maybe I'm not concentrating. Then God allows sickness to touch the life of a loved one or there is some other close personal crisis, and then I really pray. The closer the problem, the more earnest my prayers.

Time is part of our problem with hard, exhausting prayer. All of us are busy, and in business or school or housekeeping we have learned the virtues of efficiency and time management. We believe we have done well if we get the diapers folded in twenty minutes, the carpet swept in fifteen minutes, the business deal settled in five minutes. We think well of ourselves because, by handling one matter efficiently, we can get more into the day, make more progress, solve more problems, perhaps enjoy more recreation later on. Persevering prayer breaks into that very normal pattern and makes havoc of our schedules. In the back of our minds we say, What goes here? Do I have to tease God?

When our girls were little and they wanted something, I did not keep them waiting. If I thought it was good for them and within my power to provide, I did so without undue delay. I did not require them to ask and ask and ask, days on end. Why then this matter of prevailing, travailing prayer?

Several years ago Harry Ironside spoke on unanswered prayer. He said that sometimes we ask for a thing and keep asking, and there is delay because it is not God's time. The God who fits all the pieces of our lives together is working over a period of time, and our time is not necessarily His time. Central Standard Time and Heaven Wisdom Time do not always coordinate. We should not demand that they do. We should not grow frustrated over the different time zones.

Sometimes the delay means God has something better for us. Wheaton had been home to me since I was a kid in high school, and I dreaded leaving, but 1946 was God's time for that to happen. And so bidding the town and its people goodbye, I figured I'd never come back except for a visit. Nine years later the door of the chaplaincy opened at the College.

I remember one dear older saint at College Church said to me, "Evan, I always prayed that God would bring you back as our pastor, but He did something else, something better. He brought you back as chaplain." The College had no chaplain at that time. I was the first appointee, so naturally I could not have anticipated that opportunity. I could not have foreseen what God had in store. The chaplaincy fulfilled a niche in our lives as a family that we could not possibly have experienced had I been pastor of College Church, where I had served for thirteen years and which my father had served during my student days.

Dr. Ironside said there are times when God has something better for us. What seemed at first like a denial was a beneficial and loving move that taught us more about faith than we otherwise would have learned. And between our assignments in Wheaton, we were given such a challenging pastorate and such supportive fellowship in Detroit that leaving that place and returning to Wheaton was a genuine struggle for me, so close were the ties.

Sometimes delay is because of wrestling in the heavenlies. If I understand this passage aright, there was delay in the answer Daniel was seeking because satanic forces were opposing the plan of the kingdom of God. Now I'm very sure there is not one moment, not one second in the history of God's redeeming work when God could not step in and with a word from His mouth put to flight the enemy and destroy the work of Satan. But apparently in the heavenlies, as on earth, God sometimes works over a period of time in the fulfillment of His purpose.

In this chapter Daniel besought the Lord for comfort and help. And the angelic being—it makes us think of the vision of the risen Christ John saw on Patmos—came to bring him that comfort and that answer. The angel stood three weeks by the Prince of Persia, and then the Archangel Michael came and there was divine victory won in the heavenlies. And Daniel had his glorious answer in prevailing prayer, because "we wrestle not against flesh and blood, but against principalities, against powers, against the rulers of the darkness of this world, against spiritual wickedness in high places" (Ephesians 6:12).

But heavenly timing and unseen spiritual warfare are not the complete picture yet. There is also a very mystical and personal element in our prevailing prayer. At times the Spirit of God seems to urge us to just carry on, hang in there, don't let go, as if saying, "You're praying in the will of God, and don't let go until it is accomplished." At those times the process of prayer becomes a lesson for us quite apart from the content of the prayer itself. The process of drawing close to God, feeling anew His personal concern for us, His power energizing the prayers— all of this is part of the plan, part of our growth. If there were nothing to learn in the process of prayer,

God could simply grant requests on the spot. We would learn little about Him if we did not prevail in prayer.

And there are other times when we prevail in prayer and wait on God with a mystical sense of the Spirit saying, "No this is not my will." And then we stop.

My Bible teacher at Wheaton was R. A. Torrey's daughter, Edith. Oh, how many folks I have met who quote Edith. She had her father's teaching gift. Miss Torrey told us this story once in class, or she may have told it to me personally. Her father was a great man of prayer. His book on the power of prayer is one of the classics. He was on the West Coast at the time and had a daughter who was taken sick. He called together some of the elders of the church, some of his friends, and they got on their knees for a time of waiting on God, and Blanche was healed. She was thereafter a blessing to so many. When she came to Wheaton, I had the privilege of being her pastor, her family's pastor, and we are still in touch with many of the children, though Blanche was later—many years later—taken home to glory. There at that sickbed was that sense of God saying, "Carry on, keep praying." But later another daughter took ill, very ill. Torrey did what he would always do—called together a group of friends and knelt to pray. Suddenly he interrupted the meeting. "Let's stop praying," he said. "God has told me He is going to take her home to heaven." Sometimes we wrestle in prayer, and God says, "Carry on." At other times He releases us from prayer and calls us to trust Him for something more profound than even our heartfelt requests.

George Mueller once said, "I never pray with greater confidence than when I pray for the salvation of a soul." Mueller prayed constantly. He will meet thousands and thousands of people in heaven because he served and loved a powerful God and was praying for the salvation of souls Christ died for. At the time of Mueller's death, all for whom he had prayed were saved except two sons of a friend, and they were both saved later. So we prevail in prayer, and press on and carry on. Even though there is satanic opposition, we are on praying ground. Prevailing prayer makes us really search our hearts and be sure that all is on the altar—that we are in position to ask for our requests and that we are praying in the will of God.

I can understand why missionaries plead for prayer as they battle the enemy. I remember feeling a strange challenge not long ago when one missionary got up and told of the work in Korea. He reported that one church in Seoul has 150,000 members, and not just names on the roll, either. Five morning services in the great auditorium, packed every time, and weekly meetings of small groups. Then he threw out a challenge. On the other side of Korea lies Japan, less than one percent Christian after a century of heroic missionary effort. And the missionaries in Japan, you and I know, are just as dedicated as those in Korea. They are all heroes to us. Across the other way from Korea is Thailand, again with so few believers after much solid effort.

If God grants me more days to serve Him, we are going to organize some special prayer bands to zero in, like Daniel did here, to zero in on Japan and Thailand along with Korea. When you see a place that seems to be utterly resistant to the gospel, you feel the need for a prayer siege of the type Daniel used here. Then will the forces of Satan be defeated, because we serve an omnipotent God who is not willing that any should perish.

I hesitate to tell this, a very personal story. Our younger daughter has three lovely daughters. One is a little feminine edition of Dennis the Menace, but totally sweet. The middle daughter, Carolyn, a beautiful child, got Chrone's disease. She was awfully sick, with fear of leukemia. I called on her at the hospital. Olena Mae and I had given her a little necklace, a beautiful little necklace that a girl would love to wear, and she had it around her neck as she lay in bed. Outside the room our daughter Margaret was distraught. A friend of hers, a Job's-comforter type, had had a strange dream. She had dreamed that little Carolyn had died. Well, when this friend told Margaret of the dream, she became quite distraught. The friend had mentioned that in her dream was a log cabin—it was next to the house in which Carolyn lived and in the dream had died. Now there are not many log cabins around Wheaton. I know of only one—directly adjacent to Margaret's house. I remember her crying, "Oh, Daddy, I'm so frightened." I said, "Honey, let me ask you a question. Was that woman a spiritual person?" Margaret's reply was not markedly affirmative. "She had no right to speak for God, or to tell you that dream," I said. I went to my knees, and have never done so more fervently, because I realized that that dream and its so-called prophecy would hang over the family for years. Then I told Margaret an experience I had gone through years earlier.

While a pastor in Detroit, I had charge of a funeral for one of the dear families in the church. I would often drive out ahead of the procession and meet the family at the gravesite. It was a beautiful day outside, and I was out there maybe twenty minutes ahead of the others. I wandered about, and had a strange feeling: Go over and look at that grave stone there, because you are going to live as many years as the person buried there. Foolishly I walked over and looked. That person had lived fifty years, and I was then forty-eight. "Evan, you're in trouble," I said to myself. Here I had a precious wife and two dear little girls to take care of, and I realized I was in for a very miserable two years if I didn't get the victory. So I laid hold of God and asked his forgiveness for listening to that satanic voice and doing that stupid thing. I really prayed. Four years later I remembered the incident, when I was fifty-two. God had just blotted it out. I told Margaret that story in the hospital, and said, "Honey, we are going to lay hold of God. And we're not going to let that woman's dream—she was stupid to tell it anyhow— we are not going to let that woman's dream hurt your peace of heart."

That was several years ago. When we were over

the other day—our times are all in His hands—here was a beautiful trophy Carolyn had just brought back from a tennis tournament where she and another girl had won the doubles. She is today a fine student, athlete, and above all, a Christian.

Thank God, greater is He that is in us than he that is in the world.

A poem by F. W. H. Meyers on Saint Paul reads, in part,

> *So even I have thirst for his inspiring.*
> *I who have talked with him forget again?*
> *Yes, many days with sobs and with desiring*
> *Offer to God the patience and the pain.*
> *Then through the mid complaint of my confession.*
> *Then through the pang and passion of my prayer,*
> *Leaps with a start the shock of his possession,*
> *Thrills me and touches and the Lord is there.*

That's the kind of prayer I believe Daniel was offering in chapter 10, the kind we all offer during crises, the kind that draws us close to God. May it be our lifelong habit, in crisis and in calm—the fervent, prevailing prayer of a child of the Triune God.

SIX

THE
GREAT PRAYER
OF JESUS
JOHN 17

*Gracious Lord, how can it be
that Thou, whose mind is so discerning and
all-knowing, can yet love me without reserve?
We thank You that You have given
us as gifts to Your Son. May all we do in the
short years we have reflect the love
and unity of the Father, Son, and Spirit.
Amen.*

WE should take off our shoes when we come to this portion of Scripture, for the ground we stand on is holy ground. Years ago at Wheaton College our Dr. Moule was speaking from John 17 and he called it the "holy of holies" of Scripture. In a wonderful sense this is a prayer we are allowed to overhear. We sit right next to our Lord and feel the intimacy and the passion of divine love in prayer.

Years ago when I was pastor at a small church next to the campus of the University of Minnesota, I took a course in romantic poets. The instructor described the difference between prose and poetry: "Prose is heard, poetry is overheard." So many times a poem wells up feelings in the heart of the person who is meditating on a certain theme. Whether anybody reads the poem or not, the writer must express the joy or the emotion of the heart in poetic phrases. The feelings are deep and personal and have to come out. That is the kind of situation we are in when we overhear this prayer of our blessed Lord—a sacred privilege indeed.

I recall once in Minneapolis speaking with a leading liberal theologian who was telling a group of us how he was moving toward belief in the Johannine authorship of the Gospel of John. He said, "I come to that seventeenth chapter of John. Only Jesus could have prayed that prayer." And he was right. The prayer is so convincing, so convicting, that none other than Jesus could have uttered it. It is a prayer of our Lord to His Father in heaven.

In the prayer the Lord Jesus speaks of those whom God has given Him. You and I know what it is to give and to receive gifts. We know that God so loved the world that He gave his only begotten Son. But wonder of wonders, *we* are God's gift to God's Son.

You know how Christ is spoken of in Hebrews— the firstborn among many brethren. What that is going to mean in the unfolding ages of eternity you and I can only dimly dream of. Yet Jesus assures us here that God has given eternal life to all those whom God has given to Him.

Our next thought, in the third verse: "This is life eternal, that they might know thee the only true God, and Jesus Christ, whom thou hast sent." There's a special quality to eternal life—more than just duration—that is sometimes overlooked when we talk about eternity. It's that intimacy Jesus spoke of—I in Thee, Thou in me, and I in them—the union with God that Jesus knew, a union between the Father and the Son, that He wants to make happen between believers, God's gift to Him, and Himself.

That union produces a quality of life in high places or in low, in the many-talented person or the simple person.

Lincoln is one of the great names in all history. License plates from Illinois proudly say "Land of Lincoln." Some years ago Billy Graham was holding meetings in Indianapolis and wanted to mention Lincoln in his talks, so he sent for a young man from Wheaton College to help him with research on Lincoln. It was a great shock to me to find that Lincoln was not an evangelical. Perhaps he had been turned off by some of the frontier evangelism, or the influence of a skeptical law partner early in his service, I don't know. He did believe the promises about the Bible. He believed in providence, in prayer. But he was not an evangelical Christian until probably the last month before the assassin's bullet felled him. Controversial figure though he had been, something of the greatness of the man had made its impact, and still does. In the deathbed chamber, when Lincoln had breathed his last, Seward, standing beside the bed, said prophetically, "Now he belongs to the ages." Dear friends, that's what eternal life means, the life of the ages, absolutely endless. "This is life eternal, that they might know thee the only true God, and Jesus Christ, whom thou hast sent."

Dear friends, as you and I practice the presence of God, as we experience the power of God within our lives, it drives away all that is petty and mean and hateful and satanic. We all have to claim 1 John 1:9 many times in our growth in grace, but there is a quality to our lives because we belong to Him. And He is in us, and we are in Him, and we are one with the eternal God.

I was talking one time with a young man who had a very deep Christian experience, a very bad backsliding in the university, and for years thereafter a glorious comeback by the power and grace of God. In that time of skepticism, he said to me, "Evan, Jesus never claimed to be God." The Lord sent the verse to my mind: "Glorify thou me with thine own self with the glory which I had with thee before the world was." My young friend had not understood that verse before. The absolute Godhead of Christ is basic to an enduring Christian faith.

A finished work is a wonderful thing. On the cross our Lord prayed those glorious seven last words or prayers. Those last two great prayers begin, "It is finished!" In three years of public ministry our Lord finished the work God gave Him to do. When you and I face life and death and the world to come, it is so wonderful to know that our work is born with us, and we are immortal until our work is done—to be able to say "Father," a word we hesitate to utter because Jesus used it and we realize our unworthiness. "Father, I am finished with the work you gave me to do." Oh, to be able to say as we follow our Savior, "I have glorified Thee." Our historic confessions rightly call this the "chief end of man."

"That they all may be one . . . made perfect in one; and that the world may know that thou hast sent me." In a recent magazine article Carl Henry

talked about the disunity of the church, calling attention to the 3000 Christian agencies working in
Washington, and few of them pulling together. I
hope he is wrong, because Jesus said, "That they
may be one." The world is not gripped by today's
record of unity among evangelicals. How can you
and I demonstrate the unity that Jesus prayed for?
Begin with love of our brethren, sliced thick. I am
deeply upset whenever I hear of someone reading
a brother out of the kingdom because he doesn't
have quite the correct slant on eschatology or on
some other debated theological point. Debates will
go on until the Lord returns, and they ought to, for
each new statement in the debate can help us understand God's Word. But love cannot wait until all the
theological questions are answered. Love is the call
of the Lord for today. That we know as a theological
certainty.

No man did more to make Wheaton College what
it is than Herman Fischer, Jr. His father is often
called the founding father of the school because his
span of service covered fifty-three years early in the
college's history. Herman, Jr., was chairman of the
board of trustees for forty-three years. I had the
privilege of being in his Sunday school class. A
brilliant, balanced Christian mind. Nothing turned
him off more than over-dogmatism on points where
Christians can differ. He told me one time of a conversation with college president V. Raymond
Edman. Herman asked him if there were not Bible-
revering rabbis at the time of Christ who were look-
ing for the Messiah. Edman answered, "Certainly."

Then the question, "Did even one of them have it right?" President Edman thought a minute and said, "Not one." It's a humbling thought. You and I love Jesus, we believe in the Bible, we believe in man's lostness, that we must get the gospel out. There must be in our hearts a love for the brotherhood. It begins right here, in our hearts and on our lips.

It is a mystery to us, and a source of great joy, how God meets us along life's road, calls us out of the kingdom of this world and into His kingdom, and protects us from the evil—the terrible and subtle evil—that would sway us from the course. In verse 16, our Lord Jesus prays for us as citizens of the heavenly kingdom while our feet still walk upon the soil of this world. We are in the world but not under worldly power. We are made of flesh but not doomed to the dust that our bones will become. Here is the truth in which we are sanctified: union with Christ through all the steps of our lives, until face to face with Him we can sing without sin or pain. One of my most memorable experiences of the power of our Lord's prayer happened on a county road in Colorado.

Olena Mae and I seldom pick up hitchhikers. We've heard too many sad reports of strangers doing harm. But like many rules, we sometimes make exceptions.

The night before we had finished an intensive Bible conference at Winding River Ranch near Grand Lake. It had been a good week, a full one, and we were both anxious to be on our way for a few days of vacation. We left a little later than planned, but at last we were rolling down the highway—just at the right moment to spot a man thumbing a ride. He was in his middle years, clean shaven, wearing tattered jeans and carrying only a brown paper sack. Both of us felt we should stop, so I pulled the car over and invited him to ride with us. Olena Mae slid over to make room.

"What is your name, sir?" I asked, "and where are you from?"

Without hesitating, the stranger answered, "I'm Orville Pratt, from Carmel, Indiana, near Indianapolis."

"Do you have a family?"

"Oh yes, a wife and two married children. My son lives in Indianapolis, and my daughter in Wheaton, Illinois."

"Wheaton! Did you say Wheaton?"

"Yes," the man continued. "Her name is Mary Wilson, just north of Wheaton in Carol Stream."

We were amazed to find our hometown mentioned by this traveler in Colorado.

"But where are you headed?" I asked him.

"Can't tell you, 'cause I don't know myself," Orville answered. "Maybe Steamboat Springs, maybe Australia."

Our curiosity obviously aroused, we pressed for more of his story. "Does your family know about this?" I asked.

"No. I walked off my job last week and didn't tell anyone where I was going. I'm part owner of a manufacturing business. We make outdoor tool sheds. It's a good business. . . ," he said, and his voice trailed off.

Olena Mae and I sat quietly for a moment. Gently I proceeded. "Do you have a church home in Carmel?"

"I did. A good church, too. I've been a deacon and an elder there—but I'm not fit to go to church any more."

With care I ventured, "Why do you say that?"

"My daughter Mary lost her boy, a four-year-old lad. I loved him. He had a heart problem, and the specialist made a mistake. I cannot forgive that doctor, so I'm in no condition to go to church any more. It's too much, I can't face it."

Our hitchhiker friend was crying now. I assured him of our deep concern and more important, of God's great love for him. We urged him to return to his wife and home, but Orville chose to get out of the car when we turned south for the Redstone Inn. We left him there—a lonely, heartbroken man—thumbing for another ride west.

Our drive to the Inn was filled with prayer. Within minutes of our arrival, Olena Mae was on the phone.

"You don't know me," she told the voice on the other end, "but my husband and I are traveling in Colorado. Earlier this afternoon we picked up your father. . . ."

"Yes, yes, I know," Mary Wilson interrupted. "He called an hour ago. He's coming home!"

Not long after we returned to Wheaton, Orville

called to thank us for our simple advice and reminders of God's care. He wanted us to visit him, and since I was to speak in Indianapolis at an alumni chapter in the next few weeks, we arranged to spend an evening in the Pratt home. They welcomed us warmly. The next morning, a Sunday, the four of us attended their church, a warm, evangelical fellowship. After church and a delightful dinner together, Orville and I went to the cemetery where his little grandson was buried. I prayed there for Orville and his loved one, and assured him of the promised resurrection and reunion. God was there with arms around us. Later, back at his home, we all thanked God that our paths had crossed on that Colorado highway.

A chance meeting? "Holy Father," Jesus prayed, "keep through thine own name those whom thou hast given me, that they may be one, as we are."

SEVEN

KINGDOM VISION PRAYERS

MATTHEW 6:10

*Loving God, You have placed our lives
securely in Your kingdom,
and there lies our hope. For some day
all enemies will be under Your feet, and the
Son will reign, and the victory
will be complete. God of the nations, keep
us in Your effective power, to
watch and work, to serve and to witness,
until that glorious day, for Jesus' sake.*

WHEN you and I think of earthly kingdoms, we are often disappointed. We may be proud of the marvelous history of freedom we Americans have enjoyed, but we look at so much in our country that needs improving. We don't need an eagle's eyesight to see the imperfection of every earthly kingdom.

The Book of Daniel offers remarkable pictures of the four great world kingdoms: Babylonia, Medo-Persia, Greece, and Rome. Then the fifth kingdom is that stone cut out of the mountain without hands which smites the image, grinds it to pieces and blows it away like chaff from a summer's threshing. Symbols of wealth and power—gold, silver, iron, brass—but the feet are a mixture of iron and clay. Then in the seventh chapter, the four kingdoms are symbolized as ravenous beasts. Outwardly the kingdoms of this world may appear grand and mighty, yet on the inside are that greed, corruption, and selfishness that come to light against the holiness of God and the law of God given in the Scripture. Wars we thought were nobly fought turn into cruel struggles for greedy gain; laws we admired as fair and orderly turn into the old political game of protecting the powerful and taking from the weak; leaders we admired show their human side and we wonder how our loyalty could have been so quickly won.

That stone cut out of the mountain without hands is the Rock of Ages, our Lord Jesus Christ. The Son of Man comes before the Ancient of Days, and the kingdom is given to Him and to the saints of God. The kingdom of God emerges like a butterfly from a cocoon.

My study of the kingdom of God is perhaps the most thrilling of any I have made in Scripture. I grew up in the home of a congregational minister. In our church circles, at that time, the kingdom of God was another term for social action. Christians were to work to relieve pain and suffering and thereby express the values and compassion of God's kingdom. Some folks, of course, believed that social action would actually bring the kingdom to earth, that all the prophecies for a future kingdom were to be fulfilled as Christians pitched in to work toward peace and justice. On the other side of the issue were those dear brothers who saw the kingdom as wholly future, mostly ethnic, and totally due to God's intervention in history. For these Christians, the kingdom was to be a recovery of faith among the Jewish people, the church having been raptured away before the kingdom-era began.

And then I entered the ministry and began to

study the Word of God and tried to live by it. I came to see the stupendous greatness of the kingdom of God as set forth in holy Scripture. The present-but-not-yet kingdom was close to the heart of Jesus' sermons. He announced that the kingdom was at hand, and still yet to be. His own words were kingdom words, and yet He will come again in power and majesty. Such a presence and such a future gives new confidence and eagerness to my prayer: Thy kingdom come. I pray for it constantly.

The kingdom of God holds out hope for the fullness of all our aspirations: our desire to be rid of the weight of sinful temptation, our desire to live without separation from loved ones, and our desire to know and love God fully. I remember while growing up I would dream of times of family reunions. The four grandparents were there, and aunts and uncles were there, and the cousins were there. But life progressed and I came to realize that we'd never know a family reunion like that where we'd all be together and have those joyous times. Later on some were not there, and we missed them. Broken family circles. A long weekend together and our paths would separate, maybe never to meet again here. I began to be impressed with the transitoriness of every earthly thing. Then side by side with my Bible study there grew that concept of the one ultimate kingdom of God, where every blessing and every bliss will be fulfilled. Not simply a chimera, an illusion, a false dream. But absolutely the heart of the redemptive message of Holy Scripture.

A passage of Scripture I have come to love is the

great resurrection chapter of 1 Corinthians 15. You remember how Paul begins by saying that he delivered unto them first of all that which he also received, how that Christ died for our sins according to the Scriptures, how He was buried according to the Scriptures. And He rose again the third day according to the Scriptures. And the many who saw Him. Then he comes to that great concluding paragraph in which he faces the grand consummation of that resurrection, the victory of Christ over death, the overcoming of all which opposes God.

One of the greatest sermons I ever read was Andrew Murray's sermon on that day when God will be all in all. Can't you just see it: Christ at the Father's right hand, exercising His mediatorial reign over the forces of heaven and earth in the conquest of evil, and then that last day when all things— every enemy of man and God—has been put under Christ's feet, and then Christ the Son, co-eternal, co-equal with the Father, delivers up the kingdom to the Father, that God may be all in all. That's what we pray for when we pray, Thy kingdom come.

The kingdom is God's single reign which comes to us—breaks in among us—in different ways and at different times, each time revealing more of God's plan. It is God's saving will in action. Not just an idea or an intention on God's part, as if, somehow, the mind of God is at work apart from the hand of God. No, the kingdom is that ongoing plan put in motion by our loving Lord and time and time again aided and advanced by God's direct personal activity.

Strangely yet sovereignly, God has allowed frustration of His will on earth by Satan, that temporary ruler of this world. Yet kingdom power is in Christ's hands, and Satan is impotent before him. By Christ's word and obedience Satan is bound and his counter-kingdom plundered. Because Christ lived among us and died to save us, men and women may enter into the circle of God's reign, the circle of salvation, and find in their own lives a direct application of all God is doing: release from the hold of Satan and a new, effective kingdom power with all its hope and blessings. Yet not full hope and complete blessing, not yet. Satan suffers setbacks, but is not yet vanquished. Defeated he is, but not yet stopped. Satan continues his evil work, especially where the gospel is unknown, but even where it is known, even alongside the kingdom message, to seek to frustrate its success and to make its fulfillment painful. But one day, the great day of the Lord's Parousia, there will be such a glorious breakthrough of God's power as the world has never seen. The battle will be His, and the victory shared with all who belong to Him. During His glorious reign on earth He will conquer every enemy. Then, with every hostile foe underfoot, He will turn over the kingdom to the Father, and the will of God will be done perfectly and forever. That's the kingdom we have in mind when we pray, Thy kingdom come.

Think of those somber words in Job 14, "If a man die, shall he live again?" Then he says, "All the days of my appointed time, I will wait until my change, my metamorphosis, comes. Thou shalt call and I will answer, and thou shalt have a fulfillment of thy goal." That's a free translation there at the end, but it speaks of that wonderful hope of renewal and unbroken fellowship. We dream of that marvelous change, and yet only in veiled language can the Scripture point us to the marvels of that heavenly kingdom in its full expression.

Billy Sunday once told a story of a dream. It was in a meadow at night. He had taken a rest, and when he woke up the sun was shining, the sky was a beautiful clear blue. In this beautiful meadow, birds were singing and the grass was a velvet green. Flowers edged along a nearby brook. He got up and looked and there in the distance was a beautiful city. The sun was shining upon the white turrets and towers of the buildings. And he thought, *Well, I better go see where I am.*

Along the walk into the city, he noticed lots of things he wasn't used to. People were smiling and gracious. Passing some children, he interrupted their playing and said, "Children, I want to find out something. I am a stranger here, and I've noticed so many differences from the cities I am used to. As I came past the outskirts of this city, I didn't see any cemeteries."

The children said, "Sir, we have no cemeteries."

He said, "I didn't see a single hospital."

The children smiled again and said, "Sir, no one is ever sick here."

He said, "I didn't see any jails or alms houses."

They said, "No one is poor. No one is ever wicked here."

He said, "For goodness' sake, where am I?"

They said, "Sir, don't you know, you're in heaven."

God shall be all in all. That was a dream, a human description with all its limitations of the glory that shall be. Meanwhile you and I are citizens of that coming kingdom. We pray and wait and work, and one day we citizens will walk through the new heavens and new earth.

J. Wilbur Chapman used to open his campaigns with a song, "I'm a stranger here, my home is far away. Upon a golden strand. Ambassador to be in realms beyond the sea. I'm here on business for my king." Our ultimate home is heaven. Paul says in Philippians 3: "Our citizenship is in heaven, from whence we look for the Savior, who shall change these bodies of humiliation, that they may be like unto his own glorious body, according to the working of his mighty power." Again Paul said in Romans 14:17: "For the kingdom of God is not meat and drink; but righteousness, and peace, and joy in the Holy Spirit."

Our Lord told Nicodemus that the way to see and to enter the kingdom of God was through the new birth. So while we say that our ultimate citizenship is in heaven, you and I are citizens of the kingdom of heaven, living here. We have a dual citizenship. If we take seriously our heavenly citizenship, and the glorious coming of the Lord Jesus, and the kingdom to come, there will be a touch of heaven here.

I am fond of the poetry of Rupert Brooke, a brilliant young Englishman who lost his life in World

War I. He was an athlete, a man of letters, a handsome figure of a man, who went off with the British Expeditionary Force not knowing if he would return. He wrote lines something like this, not quoting exactly, but the thought of it was: "If I should die on foreign soil, and be buried there, please think that this little spot will be forever England, holding a body that was nurtured in England, bathed by her sun, breathed her air."

Where God plants you and me as citizens of the heavenly kingdom, and we live out that heavenly citizenship and work and pray for the coming of the kingdom, there's a touch of the heavenly kingdom there.

Charles Malik is a man I've long admired. He was saved through a mission school in Lebanon, rose to the presidency of the United Nations, and he was always known as a Christian, not ashamed of the gospel of Christ. He gave an address recently at Wheaton College entitled "The Two Tasks." In the introduction to his formal address, he said, "I speak to you as a Christian. Jesus Christ is my Lord and God and Savior and Song day and night. I can live without food, without drink, without sleep, without air, but I cannot live without Jesus. Without Him I would have perished long ago. Without Him and His church reconciling man to God the world would have perished long ago." Malik went on to describe his dependence on the Scriptures for daily wisdom and for insight into God's plan for the ages. "And believe me," he finished, "not a day passes without my crying from the bottom of my heart,

'Come, Lord Jesus!' I know He is coming with glory to judge the living and the dead, but in my impatience I sometimes cannot wait, and I find myself in my infirmity crying with David, 'How long, Lord?' And I know His kingdom shall have no end."

Thy kingdom come. And meanwhile, a touch of heaven—God's will be done on earth.